Hacker

Sue Leather and Julian Thomlinson

T0349320

Series Editor: Rob Waring
Story Editor: Julian Thomlinson
Series Development Editor: Sue Leather

HEINLE
CENGAGE Learning

Australia • Brazil • Japan • Korea • Mexico • Singapore • Spain • United Kingdom • United States

HEINLE
CENGAGE Learning™

Page Turners Reading Library

Hacker

Sue Leather and Julian Thomlinson

Publisher: Andrew Robinson

Executive Editor: Sean Bermingham

Senior Development Editor:
Derek Mackrell

Assistant Editor: Sarah Tan

Director of Global Marketing:
Ian Martin

Content Project Manager:
Tan Jin Hock

Print Buyer:
Susan Spencer

Layout Design and Illustrations:
Redbean Design Pte Ltd

Cover Illustration: Eric Foenander

Photo Credits:
35 Photosani/Shutterstock
36 Matthew Griffiths/Wikimedia
Commons
37 Pedro Miguel Sousa/Shutterstock

ISBN-13: 978-1-4240-4649-2

ISBN-10: 1-4240-4649-1

Heinle
20 Channel Center Street
Boston, Massachusetts 02210
USA

Cengage Learning is a leading provider of customized learning solutions with office locations around the globe, including Singapore, the United Kingdom, Australia, Mexico, Brazil, and Japan. Locate your local office at:
international.cengage.com/region

Cengage Learning products are represented in Canada by Nelson Education, Ltd.

Visit Heinle online at **elt.heinle.com**

Visit our corporate website at
www.cengage.com

Printed in the United States of America
2 3 4 5 6 7 – 14 13 12 11

Contents

Background Reading

People in the story

Jack Garcia
Jack is a computer science
student at Brenton College.

Chris Chang
Chris is Jack's friend and also
a computer science student.

Dr. Jeff Mason
Dr. Mason is head of Computer
Science. He is also on the
Brenton scholarships board.

Roberta Murtic
Roberta is Chris Chang's
friend. She studies
communications.

Professor Archibald Walker
Professor Walker is the
president of Brenton College.

This story is set in Brenton, a college town in the
northwestern United States.

Chapter 1

Jack

Jack Garcia opened the door and walked into class. He was twenty minutes late for Dr. Jeff Mason's class on computer security. It was the most difficult class of the week for most students of computer science, and the room was quiet. Jack tried not to make any noise as he came in, but the other students all turned and looked at the thin young man with long dark hair.

Dr. Mason was at the front of the class, talking. He looked up at Jack; it wasn't a good look.

"Did I miss anything?" Jack asked Chris Chang as he sat down next to him at the back of the room

Chris showed Jack some pages of computer code. "We need to find the mistakes in this," he said. His face showed that he thought it was very difficult.

"OK," said Jack, looking at the problem. "Let me see." He took out his notebook.

"Where were you anyway?" asked Chris as he turned to Jack.

"Late night," Jack said. He smiled, but his face looked tired, and he had dark circles under his eyes. Jack had to work at a burger restaurant in Brenton most nights because he needed money for college.

Chris shook his head. "Be careful, Jack," he said. "Mason was asking about you."

Jack looked at Dr. Mason. He was sitting at the front of the class reading.

"He just likes to give me a hard time," said Jack.

"Maybe," said Chris, "but you still need to finish your project this semester." All the students were doing semester projects on computer security, but Jack hadn't done much on his.

"Well, I need more time," said Jack. He made a correction in the notes in front of him.

"Remember we get our end-of-semester grades next week," Chris went on. His face was unhappy.

"He can't fail me," Jack said, his eyes moving quickly over the page. "Anyway, my average is good. I'll be fine."

"Yeah, well, like I said, he was asking about you," Chris went on. "Just so you know . . ."

Jack found another mistake and made a correction. "OK, that's done," he said.

Chris looked down at the work in front of them and then at Jack. "How did you . . . ? Why can't you finish your project as quickly?" he asked.

"Jack," said Dr. Mason as Jack and Chris were leaving the classroom. "I'd like to speak with you, please."

"See you later, Chris," Jack said. He turned to look at Dr. Mason.

"I see you were late again today," Mason said.

"I had to work some more hours at the burger restaurant," Jack replied.

"Jack, I understand," said Mason. "I know you have to work, but you still need to come to your classes. On time. Your classes are the most important thing, right? That's why you're here, isn't it?"

Mason smiled—his usual "look-at-me-I'm-a-nice-guy" smile.

Jack didn't like that smile much. In fact, he didn't like Dr. Mason that much. Dr. Mason was on the scholarships board. The board didn't give Jack a scholarship for Brenton College, and now Jack had to work to stay there. He had to work a lot.

"I'm doing the best I can," Jack said.

"Really, Jack?" Mason replied. "Are you really doing the best you can? You know, Jack, you're a smart guy. But you're failing my course this semester because you're late for classes and not working on your project. Now, really, Jack, how smart is that?"

"I *am* working on the project," Jack said. "I told you, I have to work. I don't get money from my family and I don't have a scholarship." *Because of you*, he thought to himself.

"Well, I'm looking forward to seeing it," Mason said, walking away. "Just remember, Jack, you're not the only student having to work to pay for college."

Chapter 2

Hacker

Jack was angry. It was only Monday, but the week was already going badly. There was just too much to do. There was all his other work for college, his work at the burger restaurant, and he wanted to go to The Wheel nightclub this weekend, too. He sat down at a computer in the corner of the room. *What am I going to do? How am I going to finish this project?*

The problem was he didn't have a project. He didn't even have an idea for a project.

Jack started looking at websites, first for ideas, but soon he was reading about new video games and looking at the websites he liked. Still, he couldn't stop thinking about Dr. Mason. *That guy*, he thought. *It's OK for him. But when you have to work every day to be at college it's a lot more difficult.*

Jack went to the college website. He knew Mason made this website, and the security for it. *Maybe I can hack into the college website*, Jack thought. *Write my project on that.* Maybe he could even find Mason's e-mail account and leave something just for him—a little surprise!

That sounds like fun, he thought as he began to work.

Jack knew he couldn't use his own computer to get into the college network. He didn't want anyone to find him, and he knew the best way was to hack into it from a computer in the college. He decided to use different computers around the college campus, in the computer room and in the library, and he went into the website through different accounts with different passwords. Getting into the college database wasn't easy, but after two days of work, Jack was sitting in the library looking at it. He looked around to make sure no one was watching him. He laughed to himself. *I'm the only student who can get in here and see this*, he thought. He looked through the e-mail accounts: *A, B, C . . .* all the way to *M. Mason, Jeff. Dr.* There it was. Jack looked through Mason's e-mail. There was e-mail to him from other teachers and students. *I just need to find a way of getting into his e-mail*, thought Jack to himself, *and leaving him something without using my name.*

Then he saw it. It was an e-mail about the central grades database, giving the teachers new passwords. *Grades database*, thought Jack. *That's where all our grades will be . . .* He knew that all the Brenton student grades for all subjects were there. Computer science, business, communications, everything went to this central database. *I could take a look, see what my grade average is this semester*, he thought to himself.

"Are you OK there?"

Jack jumped.

It was the computer room manager, Ms. Lee. She smiled at Jack, who was standing in front of the computer screen now. "Great," he said. "Just working on my project."

"No problem," said the manager. "Let me know if you need anything."

"Thank you," said Jack, smiling.

The manager went on walking round the room, and Jack sat down again. He opened the e-mail and saw Mason's new password. *Your new password for the main college grades database is KLJHED72*, it said.

Jack could feel his heart going very fast as he wrote the password down in his notebook. A short time later he was into the main college database and looking at the grades for all of the students at Brenton. He looked down the list of names . . . *A* . . . *B* . . . *C. This is amazing!* he thought. Before he saw his own name, he saw his friend: *Chris Chang.* Chris was failing, he saw.

Then just above it, his own name: *Jack Garcia.* Next to his name were the grades for his computer science course: *Projects, Classwork, Computer Security*— everything. Then there were grades for other subjects he had to take, and a grade for attending class. In all, there were ten grades. Some were Bs, others were Cs, but some were Fs. The important thing was the grade average. His average was D+. *Fail*, it said. All students needed a C– average to pass the course!

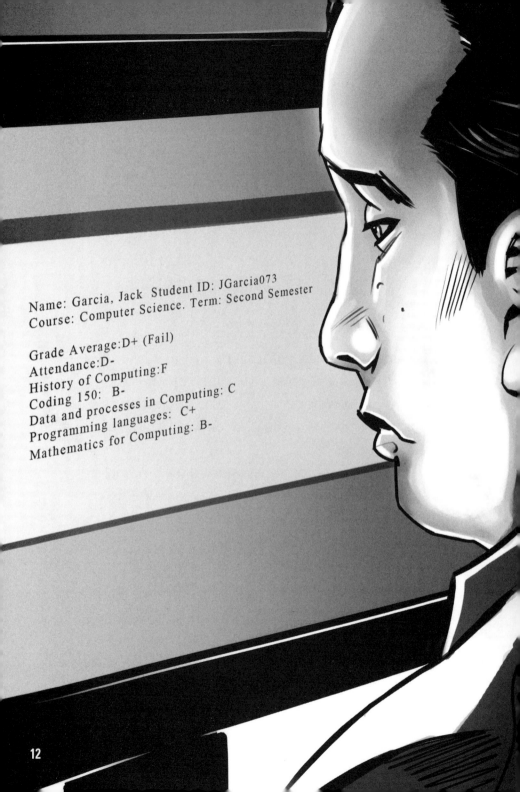

Name: Garcia, Jack Student ID: JGarcia073
Course: Computer Science. Term: Second Semester

Grade Average:D+ (Fail)
Attendance:D-
History of Computing:F
Coding 150: B-
Data and processes in Computing: C
Programming languages: C+
Mathematics for Computing: B-

Fail! What am I going to do? Jack thought. And then another thought, *I can change it.* Jack sat back in his chair and thought about it. Hacking into the database was one thing. But changing a grade? That was really serious. *But I'm failing anyway,* he told himself. *What can I lose?*

He looked at each one of his grades. His math grade was a B–. *That's no good,* thought Jack. Math was his best subject. He changed it to a B. What else? There was no grade for Projects yet. What about attendance? Jack didn't always go to class, and when he went he was often late. His grade was D–. Maybe he could change that, too? He changed it from D– to D+, and smiled as he saw his grade average go up to C–.

Pass, it said.

How about that for a security project? Jack thought to himself.

Chapter 3

Friends in need

"You did what?" Chris Chang couldn't believe what he heard.

"Shhh!" said Jack, looking round. "Don't talk so loud."

It was two days later, and the two of them were sitting and drinking coffee at the Cascade Café.

"But how . . . ?"

"Don't worry about that," Jack went on. "Just don't tell anybody." He took a drink of his coffee.

"But do you think someone will find out what you did?" asked Chris.

Jack laughed. "Well, I did it two days ago and no one seems to know." Then he saw that Chris looked serious and Jack said, "No, I was careful. I made very small changes, instead of making one big one. And the teachers don't look at the average."

They drank their coffee for a few minutes. Chris looked worried. Neither of them spoke. Then Chris said, "Did you see my grades?"

Jack didn't say anything.

"Jack?"

"Yeah, I saw them," Jack replied. "You have a D."

Chris dropped his head.

Jack looked at Chris's unhappy face. Jack didn't have many friends in college. Just Chris, really.

Chris looked up at him, about to speak.

"Don't ask, Chris," Jack said. "Let me see what I can do."

"Hey, thanks, Jack," Chris replied. "You're a real friend."

The next day, Jack went back into the grades database and changed Chris's grade to a C–. He was very careful, but for a few days after, he was worried. He felt like someone was watching him. To say thank you, Chris took him to The Wheel nightclub in the city on Saturday night. Chris brought some friends of his— Pete Chandling and Roberta Murtic and some others. They played good music at The Wheel; Jack, Chris, and the others all danced. Jack was having a *great* time.

At about ten o'clock, Jack felt very hot from all the dancing and he went to get a drink. As he was coming back to the dance floor, Roberta walked up to him. She was a short young woman with beautiful clothes, a first-year student. Like Pete Chandling, she studied communications.

"Hey, Jack."

"Hey Roberta, how's it going?"

"Oh, OK," she said. "Can I talk to you, Jack?"

"Yeah, sure, let's sit down," he said.

They sat down at a table away from the music. Roberta looked at him.

"You know, we haven't talked much, have we?" Roberta began.

"Well, no, I guess not," Jack said.

"Pete says you're a really nice guy," Roberta said. *Did he?* thought Jack.

"We could be friends," Roberta said.

How about that? Jack thought. *First the grades, and now some new friends. And Roberta's pretty, too. What a great week . . .*

"The thing is, Jack," she said, "I know I'm going to fail my course and my mom's going to be really angry . . ." She looked more worried as she spoke about it.

Jack knew from Chris that Roberta's mother had a TV company and wanted her to study communications.

Why is she telling me this? Jack asked himself. But he knew the answer.

He looked at Roberta. "You talked to Chris," he said.

Roberta nodded her head. "Yes," she said quietly. "But only because he's a friend . . . he didn't mean to . . ."

Chris and his big mouth, thought Jack. *I told him not to tell anyone!*

"The answer's 'no.' I can't," Jack said. "I mean, they changed the password. I can't get into the database now."

This wasn't true, but he didn't want people talking about him changing grades. *What were you thinking, Chris?* he thought.

"I see. Chris was saying you worked at Burger Time," Roberta went on. "And that you don't have much money."

"So?" Jack asked.

"I thought maybe I could give you some money, you know, if you help me?"

"Hey!" Jack said, getting up. He was angry. *This is the problem with people with money,* he thought. *They can always buy their way out of trouble.*

"Sorry, Jack. I didn't mean to make you angry," Roberta said. "Please think about it, OK? This is really important for me."

Jack thought about it.

"I'll do it for a thousand dollars." He said it as a joke. *That'll make her go away,* he thought.

"OK," Roberta said.

"What?" said Jack. "Are you serious?"

"Sure, I'm serious. I'll give you a thousand dollars if you do it. Here's my number," she said, giving him a piece of paper.

"I . . . I need to think about it," Jack said.

"Jack, come on. A thousand dollars. How many hours at Burger Time is that?" Roberta asked him.

"Two hundred" was the answer. A thousand dollars was two hundred hours of work at Burger Time. Ten weeks at twenty hours a week. With money like that, he could really study hard. It was wrong, he knew. But it wasn't hurting anyone. *Anyway*, he thought, *isn't this how people get money in the first place?*

"I'll do it," he said. "But you must promise me one thing. You can't tell anyone about this. Do you understand? Not one person."

"Oh, Jack, you're so cool. Thank you so much."

"Did you hear what I said? You mustn't . . ."

". . . tell anyone. Yes, I understand. So you'll do it, then? Oh, you're a real friend, Jack."

Friend, Jack thought.

"Yeah, I'll do it," he said.

That was when it all went wrong.

Chapter 4

Small business

The next day, Jack went onto the grades database in the college library. He found Roberta's grade. It was an F.

An F? Jack thought. *That's a big change—an F to a D. Maybe too big.*

He thought about it. D to C wasn't a big thing. But an F—Roberta was really failing the course. But then he thought about the money. *$1,000.*

He changed the grade.

I have a bad feeling about this, he thought, as he turned off the computer.

"Hi, Jack!"

Jack turned around fast. It was Dr. Mason.

"Dr. Mason," Jack said. "I . . . I didn't know you were there."

It was difficult for Jack to speak. *Did he see?* Jack thought. *This could be the end.*

"I guess you're working on your project, eh?" Mason said. "Going OK?"

"What? The project? Oh, yes. The project. I'm working on the project, that's right."

"Are you all right, Jack?" Mason asked him. "Your face is white."

"I'm fine," Jack replied. "Just . . . tired."

"Is there anything you'd like to talk about?" Mason asked. He smiled as he said it.

"No, I don't think so," Jack said.

"Are you sure? Nothing at all?"

"No, nothing," Jack said. "Everything's cool."

"Good," Mason said. "That's good, Jack. Well, I'll see you in class."

"Yes. Thanks, Dr. Mason."

Mason looked at Jack before he left. It was a strange look, Jack thought.

Does he know? Did he see something?

No, that's impossible.

Jack watched Mason walk away, then went quickly out of the library.

After lunch, Jack went to meet Roberta in the Cascade Café so she could give him the money. She was sitting waiting for him, but two other students were with her. Jack didn't know them. *What are they doing here?* he thought. He sat down at a table on the other side of the café and asked for a coffee. Roberta saw him a minute later and came over.

"Jack!" she said. "Why are you sitting over here?"

"Because you've got friends with you, of course. Have you got the money?"

"Sure. Sure. It's here." She gave it to him, and he put it quickly into his pocket.

"What are you doing?" Jack asked. "Why did you bring those two with you?"

"My friends, well, I thought maybe you could help them."

"What?!" Jack stood up.

"Take it easy, Jack. They're cool. I know you said not to tell anyone," Roberta went on, "but they're really nice guys. If you just talk to them, you'll see."

"Listen to me, Roberta," Jack said. "Don't you understand how dangerous this is? You promised not to tell!"

"I know, but if you just talk to them . . ."

"No, I won't talk to them. And don't speak about this to anyone else. You promise me now!"

"Jack, I . . ."

"Promise!"

"I'm sorry. I promise, Jack. I won't tell anyone."

But it seemed Roberta didn't keep her promise. Over the next few days, a number of students came to him and asked him to change their grades. They found him

walking around the campus or in the library. One even came to his room.

He said no to everyone, told them all to keep quiet, but they still came to him. Jack was angry. But he was also worried. Too many people were talking. But what could he do? *Nothing*, he thought. He couldn't sleep because he was thinking about it, and he found it difficult to listen in his classes.

He found Roberta walking through the college near the library. He walked up next to her and took her arm.

"I want to speak to you," he said. "You agreed to be quiet. But people are coming to me all the time, asking me to change their grades!"

"Jack!" she said. "No, I didn't tell anyone. I really didn't. And I told my friends not to say anything."

"You did. You told people! You agreed not to."

"Jack, I didn't tell anyone! Really! Hey, let go of my arm. Let go of me!"

She pulled away from him. Jack saw he was holding her arm too tightly.

"I'm sorry," he said. "I'm really sorry."

He walked away quickly. Maybe it wasn't Roberta. But if it wasn't her, then who was it? The only other person was Chris.

"Oh, maybe I told one or two people, now that I think about it," Chris said, back at his room.

"Chris!" Jack said. "This is bad. Really bad."

"I thought you could make some money. You're always talking about not having any. Anyway, listen. The college doesn't know. Mason doesn't know. So just forget about it. People will stop asking you soon."

Chris was right. People stopped asking. But Jack was still worried. He was too worried to sleep, too worried to study. He had the $1,000 from Roberta, but he was too worried to use it. He was so worried he forgot all about his semester project.

Chapter 5

The last time

"I'm sorry," Dr. Mason said. "I can't give you any more time, Jack. I'll have to give you an F."

"Just one more week. It's almost finished."

"You know I can't do that, Jack," Mason said.

Jack sat down and put his head in his hands. It was nearly the end of the semester, and Jack was sure an F in Projects would make him fail the whole course.

"I know this is a big thing," Mason went on. "I'll check your grade average after the class. If you are failing, we'll need to have another talk. You'll need to do the semester again."

Check my grade average?! Jack knew what he needed to do. He had to change his grade before Mason looked at the database. He sat at the front so he could leave class early. When it finished, he ran to the computer room. It was dangerous, but what could he do?

The manager looked at him and smiled as he walked in. *I have to be quick,* he thought. As usual, he put in the password *K . . . L . . . J . . . H . . . E . . . D . . . 7 . . . 2.*

The computer was going slowly. *Why is this taking so long?* he thought. At first, he couldn't find his name. It was hard to think. Minutes went by. Jack started to feel very hot. He could hear the clock now. Then, yes! There it was. He found his name at last. *Project: F,* it said. He couldn't change that, he knew, so he changed his other grades to give him a C– average. *That's it,* he thought. *I did it! I can go!*

He got his things and went outside. Dr. Mason was standing just outside the door, with two of the college's security men.

"Come with me, Jack," Mason said.

"We knew for some time," said Dr. Mason. "I think everybody in college knew—so many people were talking about it. But we needed to catch you using my password and changing a grade."

Jack didn't speak. He was sitting with Dr. Mason in the president's office. The president, Professor Walker, was listening carefully.

"We have the CCTV video, too," Mason continued.

"The CCTV video?" Walker asked.

"The video of people who were in the computer room at the time," Mason said.

"I see."

Again, Jack didn't speak.

"What do you think happens now, Jack?" Professor Walker asked him.

Jack knew. He knew he couldn't stay at college.

"You mean I have to leave the college?"

As he said it, Jack suddenly thought that having to leave college wasn't so bad. He wasn't having a good time there. *And lots of smart guys don't finish college,* he thought. *Look at Bill Gates.* Jack started to think about everything he could do outside college. *Just like Bill Gates,* he thought. *Maybe I can make some real money like him.* No, having to leave college didn't seem so bad. *And I'll still have my friends,* he thought.

Walker and Mason looked at each other.

"He really doesn't understand, does he, Jeff?" Walker asked.

Understand what? Jack thought.

Professor Walker picked up his phone. "Please ask them to come in now," he said.

Ask who?

"Are you sure about this?" Mason asked Walker. "Jack's not so bad. He's just, well, very young. He's still just a boy, Archie."

"Jeff, we have to do this, you know that," Professor Walker answered,

Do what? Jack thought, but then the door opened, two police officers walked in, and he understood.

"Jack Garcia," one of the officers began, "you're under arrest."

"We have a record of the changed grades," Mason went on. "All your friends will have to leave college, too. You know that, don't you, Jack?"

Jack's mouth fell open. He didn't know what to say. He suddenly felt hot, and felt like crying.

"Please don't do this," he said.

One police officer stood Jack up and put his hands in handcuffs. The other officer continued to read him his rights as they took him from the room.

"Please, you don't have to do this. I can change them back. The grades. I'll change them back, like they were before. Please!"

The police officers didn't reply. Jack looked back. Dr. Mason watched him go from the room. He shook his head and closed the door.

Review

A. Match the characters in the story to their descriptions.

1. _____ Jack Garcia

2. _____ Chris Chang

3. _____ Dr. Jeff Mason

4. _____ Roberta Murtic

5. _____ Professor Walker

a. a first-year communications student, Chris's friend

b. a computer science student, Jack's only friend

c. president of Brenton College

d. a computer science student who works part-time

e. the head of Computer Science

B. Read each statement and circle whether it is true (T) or false (F).

1. Jack is better than Chris at computer science.   T / F

2. Dr. Mason cares about how well Jack is doing in school.   T / F

3. Jack uses his own laptop computer to get into the college network.   T / F

4. Chris offers Jack some money to change his grades.   T / F

5. Jack does not know Roberta Murtic very well.   T / F

6. Roberta was failing her communications course badly.   T / F

7. Jack helps a few more people change their grades.   T / F

8. Dr. Mason does not want Professor Walker to call the police.   T / F

C. Choose the best answer for each question.

1. What is the main reason Jack doesn't like Dr. Mason?

a. He thinks Dr. Mason is the reason he didn't get a scholarship.

b. He knows Dr. Mason doesn't like him.

c. He feels Dr. Mason always gives him a hard time.

d. He thinks Dr. Mason does not need to worry about money.

2. Where does Jack work?

a. Cascafe Café

b. the computer lab

c. The Wheel nightclub

d. Burger Time restaurant

3. What is the main reason Roberta talks to Jack at the nightclub?

a. She wants to be friends with him.

b. She wants to ask him to dance with her.

c. She wants him to help change her grades.

d. She wants to thank him for helping Chris.

4. Why does Jack fail his project in the end?

a. He did not study hard enough.

b. He was busy spending his money.

c. He was busy changing grades for other people

d. He worried so much that he forgot all about it.

5. Why does Dr. Mason only catch Jack much later?

a. He was waiting for Jack to tell him.

b. He was waiting for one of Jack's friends to tell him.

c. He needed to catch Jack in the act of hacking.

d. He wants to see if Jack will pass his computer course.

D. Complete each sentence with the correct word from the box.

network	database	scholarship	e-mail
grade	project	semesters	password

1. A(n) _____ is a piece of work that takes a lot of time and effort.

2. A(n) _____ is a special code to enter a place or computer system.

3. A(n) _____ is a written message that is sent electronically.

4. If you get a(n) _____, your studies are paid for by the school or an organization.

5. A school year is usually divided into two periods of time, or _____.

6. A(n) _____ is a connection of many computers together.

7. A(n) _____ is a collection of information stored on a computer.

8. A(n) _____ is a mark that shows how well you've done on your test.

Background Reading:

Spotlight on ... *Hackers*

Hackers are people who are very good with computers—they write software (computer programs) and often know several computer languages.

In movies and books, a hacker is a person who breaks into computers and computer networks. They usually try to steal money or valuable information, but some do it just for fun.

But not all hackers are bad. Many are actually hired by computer security firms to hack into their systems and test how safe they are. These people are known in the business as "white hats." The hackers that break into networks or create viruses are called "black hats."

Kevin Poulsen started hacking from a young age. When he was 17 years old, he hacked into the U.S. Department of Defense's computer system, and continued breaking into government systems in the 1980s. The police wanted to arrest Poulsen because he had access to top-secret information.

His most famous hack was to take over all the telephone lines for a radio station in Los Angeles, California. The station was holding a contest to give away a fancy car to the 102nd caller. All Poulson had to do was make sure he was the 102nd caller, and then collect his new car!

Poulsen was finally arrested in 1991. He paid a $56,000 fine and spent almost five years in prison. He was also not allowed to touch a computer for three years after his release.

Today, Poulsen is no longer a hacker. He is a respected journalist and editor at Wired News, an online technology news website.

Think About It

1. Is it always bad to break into another computer?

2. Has your computer ever been hacked? How did it make you feel?

Spotlight on ... *Internet Security*

Many of us do not think twice about using the Internet for just about everything. This has led to the number of computer crimes increasing over the last few years. A criminal may be able to access important information by stealing passwords and breaking into  online accounts, and people may not find out until much later.

So how can we protect ourselves? Here are some tips:

- Change your password often.
- Never reveal your password to anyone.
- Use a combination of letters and numbers for your password.
- Use different passwords for different websites.
- Make copies of your important data and information often.
- Make sure you have Internet security software and are using the latest version.
- Remove any information you don't want others to find on your computer.
- Only download things from websites that you trust.
- Read the privacy messages of websites you join or software you put in your computer.
- Know that other people's computers may not be as safe as yours.

Most Popular Internet Passwords
1. 123456
2. 12345
3. 123456789
4. password
5. iloveyou
6. princess
7. rockyou
8. 1234567
9. 12345678
10. abc123
(Source: NYT/Imperva)

Think About It

1. Have you ever had a computer virus? What happened?

2. Why do you think so many people use the top 10 passwords even though they are easy to guess?

Glossary

average	(*n.*)	the average of 1+8+7+4 is 5 (20/4=5)
campus	(*n.*)	the buildings and grounds of a college
computer code	(*n.*)	computer language
cool	(*adj.*)	someone who is fashionable or attractive
correction	(*n.*)	If you make a correction, you make something that was wrong right again.
database	(*n.*)	a big store of information on a computer
e-mail account	(*n.*)	the place online where you send and get e-mails. For example your e-mail account address may be me@xyz.com.
fail	(*v.*)	If you fail a course, you do not pass and have to take it again.
grade	(*n.*)	Your grade for a course at college is your score, such as A–, B+, or C.
library	(*n.*)	a building or room where books are kept
network	(*n.*)	a connection of many computers together
notebook	(*n.*)	You write down notes in a notebook.
project	(*n.*)	a classroom activity over a long period of time, e.g., making a class newspaper
promise	(*v.*)	If you tell someone you will do something, you are promising to do it.
scholarship	(*n.*)	money paid by a college to students for special reasons
security	(*n.*)	Computer security keeps the computers safe from people breaking into them and stealing data.
semester	(*n.*)	a period of about 15 weeks of study time at college. Most colleges in the U.S. have two semesters a year.
smart	(*adj.*)	very clever
task	(*n.*)	an activity or a piece of work